Aesop's Fables

retold by *Ann McGovern*

Inside illustrations by *A.J. McClaskey*

AN
APPLE
PAPERBACK

SCHOLASTIC INC.
New York Toronto London Auckland Sydney

ISBN 0-590-43880-8

36 35 34 33 3፣   8 9/9 0 1/0

Printed in the U.S.A.   40

Contents

The Fox and the Grapes

A HUNGRY Fox stole into a vineyard one day. There he saw bunches of sun-ripened grapes hanging high on the vine. They looked so plump and juicy he could hardly wait to eat them. He jumped up to seize the nearest bunch of grapes, but they were too high and he could not reach them.

He jumped again and again. But again and again he missed. At last he looked up at the grapes and walked away, saying, "Anyone can see that those grapes are sour." Which proves, of course, that *it is easy to despise what you know you cannot possess.*

The Donkey in the Lion's Skin

A DONKEY once found the skin of a Lion and dressed himself in it. Then he amused himself by roaming about in the forest, frightening all the animals he met. When he saw the Fox, he tried to frighten him too. But as soon as the Fox heard the Donkey bray, he said, "Ah, my friend, I might have been frightened like the others if I had not heard your voice. *Clothes may disguise a fool until he opens his mouth.*"

The Hunter
and the Woodsman

ONE day a Hunter was looking for the tracks of a Lion. In his search, he came upon a Woodsman felling oaks in the forest.

"Pray tell me," the Hunter said to the Woodsman, "have you seen the marks of the Lion's footsteps? Or perhaps you can tell me where his den is?"

"I will do better than tell you," the Woodsman replied courteously. "I will take you right to him."

The Hunter turned pale. His teeth began to chatter. "N-o thank you," he said. "I did not ask for *that!* It is only his tracks that I am in search of, not the Lion himself."

"I see," said the Woodsman. "You call yourself a hunter of lions. But *a hero must be brave in deed as well as in word.*"

The Falconer and the Partridge

A FALCONER one day discovered a Partridge in the nets he had set out to trap some birds. As he approached his prey, the bird cried out, "Please, sir, let me go. If you but free me, I promise you I will lure many other Partridges into your nets."

"No," replied the Falconer. "I might have set you free, but you well deserve your fate. For *to betray ones friends to save oneself is a vile crime.*"

The Man and the Lion

A MAN and a Lion were traveling together through the forest. They began to argue as to who was the stronger — man or lion. In the midst of their quarrel they passed a stone statue which showed a man strangling a lion.

"There!" said the Man, pointing to the statue. "See how strong man is! Does this not prove that I am right?"

The Lion chuckled. "Ah," he said, "but this statue was made by a man. If we Lions knew how to build statues, you would see *that* man under the paw of *that* lion. *How a story ends often depends on the storyteller.*"

The Hare and the Hound

ONE day a Hound came upon a Hare resting under a bush. At once the Hound gave chase, but as fast as he ran the Hare ran faster and soon escaped. A passing Shepherd saw how the Hound had lost the Hare. He called out scornfully, "You call yourself a hunter? Why, that Hare was one tenth your size and still he got away from you!"

"Ah," said the Hound, "you forget that I was only running for my supper, while the Hare was running for his life. It is ever true that *fear lends wings to the feet.*"

The Stag at the Pool

ONE summer's day a Stag came to a clear spring to drink. As he bent his head, he saw his image in the clear water. "Ah," he thought, tossing his head proudly, "how very handsome are my antlers." He peered closer, and then said with despair, "But my legs and my feet are another matter! Oh, how weak, how slender they are!"

So absorbed was the Stag in his own image that he did not hear the approach of the Lion until the beast was about to spring. Just in time, however, the Stag ran away. It seemed as if the Stag would escape his pursuer, for as long as he was on the open plain he was able to outrun the Lion. But then the Stag entered a forest and, in his swift flight, caught his antlers in the branches of the trees. And the more he tried to free himself, the more entangled his antlers became.

In a few moments the Lion was upon him. Too late, the Stag reproached himself: "Woe is me! How I have deceived myself! I scorned the feet which would have saved me and praised the antlers which have caused my downfall. *Too often we despise what we should value most.*"

The Farmer and the Stork

A FARMER placed nets on his newly planted fields and caught a number of Cranes that had come to pick his corn seed. Among the Cranes there was one Stork.

"Pray spare me, master," begged the Stork, "And let me go free this once. I am no Crane, but a Stork of excellent character. Look at my feathers, my legs, and my beak. You can see that in no way do they resemble those of the Cranes."

The Farmer was not moved by these words. "All that you say may be true," he said, "but I caught you with these robbers and have every reason to think you are a robber, too. After all, *birds of a feather flock together*."

The Ant and the Grasshopper

ONE fine summer's day, a Grasshopper was chirping and singing as if he had not a care in the world. An Ant passed by, struggling with a kernel of corn which he was carrying to his nest.

The Grasshopper called to the busy Ant, "Come and visit with me for a while. It is far too nice a day to be working."

The Ant looked at the Grasshopper. "I observe you do nothing but sing all day," he said. "I do not have time to sing and play. I am storing up food for the long winter days ahead, and I suggest you do the same."

The Grasshopper laughed and said, "Why worry about winter? I have enough food for the present."

Months passed. The snow lay on the fields. The Ant was content. In his house there was food to last all winter. But the Grasshopper had nothing to eat. "Ah," he said sadly, "I am dying of hunger. If only I had realized that *it is best to prepare today for the needs of tomorrow.*"

The Donkey, the Rooster, and the Lion

A DONKEY and a Rooster lived peaceably together in the farmyard. One day a hungry Lion passed by. His eyes brightened at the sight of the plump Donkey, and he thought of the fine meal in store for him.

But just as the Lion was about to pounce on the Donkey, the Rooster began to crow. Now, it is said there is nothing a lion hates more than the sound of a cock-a-doodle-doo. Perhaps it is true, for the Lion turned and fled at the sound of the Rooster's crowing.

The Donkey laughed. "Why, the Lion is a coward! The mighty King of Beasts runs from a rooster." And the Donkey felt so bold that he began to chase the Lion. He had not gone very far, however, when the Lion turned. With a great roar, he leaped upon the Donkey.

The Rooster, watching from the farmyard, said sadly, "Alas, my poor friend did not realize what he could or could not do. *False confidence often leads to misfortune.*"

The Fox Without a Tail

ONE day a Fox, running through the woods, was caught in a trap. He managed to escape with his life, but lost his handsome bushy tail. Ashamed of the way he now looked, he hid in the forest, where no one could see him.

In this way he passed the days, thinking how could he ever face the other foxes?

Then one day he had an idea. He ran into the clearing where the foxes were gathered and cried loudly, "Look at me, dear friends. Observe that I no longer have my tail! How wonderful it is to be free of all that heavy fur! And see how it improves my appearance! Since all of you are my brothers, I would like you to be as carefree as I am. I myself am ready now to cut off your tails!"

"Brother Fox," said one of the wise old foxes, "tell me, if you had not lost your own tail, would you be so ready to help us get rid of ours? Are you not eager to see us without tails because you know that *misery loves company?*"

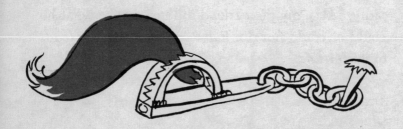

The Lion and the Boar

ONE hot summer's day a Lion and a Boar came to a small well at the same moment. They were both very thirsty, and began at once to argue as to who should be the first to drink. Neither would give in to the other. They were about to come to blows when the Lion looked up and saw some vultures in the sky above them.

"Look!" said the Lion. "Those vultures see us fighting and they are hungry. They are waiting to feed upon the loser."

"Then let us settle our quarrel," said the Boar. "It is better for us to make friends than to become the food of vultures."

"I agree," the Lion said. *"In the face of common danger, small differences are best forgotten."*

Jupiter and the Bee

THE Queen Bee once wished to offer a gift of honey to Jupiter. She collected the freshest honey from her honeycombs and flew with it up to Mount Olympus. The god was so delighted with this gift that he promised to give the Queen Bee anything she asked. "All-powerful Jupiter," said the Queen Bee, "I beg of thee, grant me a sting so that I may kill whoever approaches my hive to steal my honey."

Jupiter was shocked that the Queen Bee would wish to revenge the theft of her honey in this way. But he could not take back his promise. So he said, "You shall have your sting. And when you attack anyone who takes your honey, the wound shall be fatal."

The Queen Bee was about to thank Jupiter. But he held up his hand and continued, "The wound shall be fatal — but only to *you!* Once you use your sting, it shall be torn from you, and you will die from the loss of it."

Thus did the Queen Bee learn that *evil wishes have evil consequences.*

Dog in the Manger

A DOG, looking for a comfortable place to nap, came upon the empty stall of an Ox. There it was quiet and cool, and the hay was soft. The Dog curled up on the hay and was soon fast asleep.

A few hours later the Ox lumbered in from the fields. He had worked hard and was looking forward to his dinner of hay. His heavy steps woke the Dog, who jumped up in a great temper. As the Ox came near the stall, the Dog snapped angrily, as if to bite him. Again and again the Ox tried to reach his food, but each time he tried the Dog stopped him.

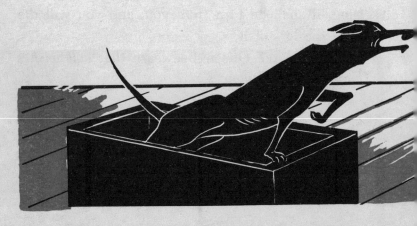

At last the patient Ox spoke up. "You do not want to eat my dinner, nor will you let me have it. *I fear there are always those who begrudge to others what they themselves cannot enjoy.*"

The Crow and the Pitcher

A CROW, who was almost dying of thirst, came upon a pitcher which had once been filled with water. But to his dismay the Crow found that the water was so low he could not reach it. He tried with all his might to knock the pitcher over, but it was too heavy.

Then he saw a pile of pebbles nearby. He took one pebble in his beak and dropped it into the pitcher. The water rose a tiny bit. Then he took another pebble and dropped that in. The water rose a tiny bit more. One by one he dropped in all the pebbles. When he had dropped in a hundred pebbles, the water at last rose to the top. As the Crow drank deeply of the cool water, he said to himself, *"Where force fails, patience will often succeed."*

The Porcupine and the Moles

IT WAS growing cold, and a Porcupine was looking for a home. He found a most desirable cave, but saw that it was occupied by a family of Moles.

"Would you mind if I shared your home for the winter?" the Porcupine asked the Moles.

The generous Moles consented, and the Porcupine moved in. But the cave was small, and every time the Moles moved around they were scratched by the Porcupine's sharp quills. The Moles endured this discomfort as long as they could. Then at last they gathered courage to approach their visitor. "Pray leave," they said, "and let us have our cave to ourselves once again."

"Oh no!" said the Porcupine. "This place suits me very well. If you Moles are not satisfied, I suggest that *you* leave!"

The poor Moles thus had to make the best of a bad situation, realizing sadly that *it is well to know one's guest before offering him hospitality.*

Hercules and the Wagoner

A WAGONER was driving his wagon along a country lane when the wheels suddenly sank into a deep rut. The Wagoner climbed down and stood looking helplessly at the wagon. Without attempting to lift the wagon out of the rut, he began to pray to Hercules, the god of strength, to come to his aid.

Hercules heard the Wagoner's cries for help. He called down from Mount Olympus: "Put your shoulder to the wheel, my man, before you pray to me for help. It is well to *try to help yourself before you ask help of others.*"

The Wolf and the House Dog

ONE evening a Wolf met a big, well-fed House Dog. He saw that the Dog wore a heavy collar around his neck, and he asked, "Who is it that feeds you so well, yet burdens you with so heavy a collar?"

" 'Tis my master," the House Dog replied.

"I would not change places with you, my friend," the Wolf said, "nor wear your collar for any master, no matter how well he fed me. The weight of the collar would spoil the appetite. *Half a meal in freedom is better than a full meal in bondage.*"

The Two Travelers
and the Ax

TWO men were traveling together on a road. Suddenly one of them bent down to pick up something that was lying on the ground. "Look!" he said, "I found an ax!"

"No, my friend," replied the other. "Do not say '*I* found an ax.' What you should say is '*We* found an ax.'"

They had not gone far when they heard a great shout. They looked back to see the owner of the ax pursuing them.

The man who had picked up the ax said, "Alas, we are in trouble."

"Oh no!" replied his friend. Do not say '*We* are are in trouble.' What you should say is '*I* am in trouble.' *If you do not want to share the prize, then do not expect to share the danger.*"

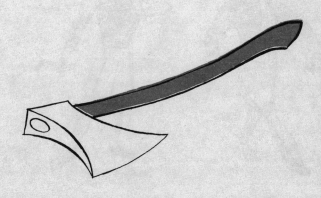

The Boastful Traveler

A YOUNG MAN who had traveled to foreign lands returned one day to his native country. There he boasted of the marvelous feats he had performed in the places he had visited.

One story he told over and over to anyone who would listen. "When I was in Rhodes," he would say, "I made the most amazing leap. Why, no man ever jumped that high! I have witnesses to prove it, too."

At last one of the townsmen who had heard this story many times said, "If what you say is true, you need no witnesses. Instead of telling us how high you leap, why not show us? *Deeds are far more convincing than boasts!*"

The Fox and the Goat

A FOX fell into a deep well and could not find a way to get out. A thirsty Goat, coming to drink at the same well, saw the Fox. "Friend Fox," the Goat said in surprise, "what are you doing down there?"

The Fox thought it best to conceal his unhappy plight. "Ah," he replied, "I could not resist this excellent water. You have never tasted such fresh, clear water in all your life. I had intended to drink it up myself, but since you are a friend I will save some for you."

The Goat was so thirsty that he jumped into the well without a second thought. Then the Fox, just as quickly, leaped upon the Goat's back. Holding onto her long horns, he was able to reach the top of the well safely.

"Wait!" cried the Goat. "Help me out too."

The Fox called down, "If you had as many brains in your head as you have hairs in your beard, you would never have gone down before you had inspected the way up. I'll help you out this time, but in the future *look before you leap.*"

27

The Fox
and the Woodcutter

A FOX was being chased by a pack of hounds. Panting, he ran up to a Woodcutter who was chopping wood outside his hut.

"Please, kind sir," begged the Fox. "Can you help me to hide until the hounds pass by?"

The Woodcutter told him to take shelter in his own hut, and the grateful Fox ran inside and hid in a corner under the window.

A few minutes later the Huntsman rode up with his hounds and asked the Woodcutter if he had seen a Fox.

The Woodcutter replied in a voice loud enough for the Fox to hear: "No, I have not seen a Fox all morning." But even as he spoke, he winked and pointed to the hut where the Fox was hiding. The Huntsman, however, did not understand these gestures and rode off, still pursuing the Fox.

As soon as the Huntsman had gone, the Fox came out of the hut. He started off without a word to the Woodcutter.

"You ungrateful fellow," the Woodcutter called after him. "You owe your life to me, yet you leave without a word of thanks."

"I would have thanked you with all my heart," the Fox replied, "if your deed had been as kind as your words. But your hands made a lie of your speech! So I cannot thank you, for *there is as much mischief in a wink as in a word.*"

29

The Shepherd and the Wolf

A SHEPHERD once found a young Wolf which had been abandoned by its mother. The Shepherd took the Wolf home and cared for it. After a while he began to teach the Wolf to steal lambs from the neighboring flocks. The Wolf proved to be such a good pupil that one day he stole a sheep from the Shepherd's own flock.

The Shepherd reproached him bitterly. But the Wolf said, "Was it not you who taught me to steal? *If you teach evil, you must expect evil.*"

The Dog and the Shadow

A DOG with a piece of meat in his mouth was crossing a bridge over a stream. Looking down, the Dog saw his own shadow in the water. Thinking that the reflection was a bigger Dog with a piece of meat twice the size of his own, the greedy Dog meant to have that, too.

Snarling, he opened his mouth to attack the enemy. At that moment his own meat fell into the stream and floated away.

Now the Dog realized at last that what he had seen was nothing but a shadow. Sadly, he said to himself, *"Grasp at the shadow and lose the substance."*

The Hares and the Frogs

FOR A long time the Hares believed that every creature of the animal kingdom was their enemy. After a while they became so tired of their many fears and worries that they decided to put an end to themselves and their troubles. They planned to drown themselves in a nearby lake, and one day they gathered sadly at the water's edge. As they were about to throw themselves into the water, the Hares noticed that all the Frogs who had been lying on the banks of the lake were rushing in great fright into the deep water for safety.

One of the wise old Hares called out to his companions. "Stop. Let us not be too hasty. Our case is not so desperate after all. See, here are other poor creatures more timid than we. It seems *there is always someone worse off than ourselves.*"

The Shepherd Boy
and the Wolf

DAY after day, a Shepherd Boy tended a flock of sheep in the hills above his village. One day, just to cause some excitement, the Shepherd Boy ran down from the hills shouting, "Wolf! Wolf!"

The townsfolk came running with sticks to chase the Wolf away. All they found was the Shepherd Boy, who laughed at them for their pains.

Seeing how well his trick worked, the Shepherd Boy tried it again the next day. Again he ran down from the hills shouting, "Wolf!" Again the townsfolk ran to his aid in vain.

But the day after, it happened that a Wolf really came. The Shepherd Boy, now truly alarmed, shouted, "Help! Come and help me! The Wolf is killing the sheep!"

But this time the townsfolk said, "He won't fool us again with *that* trick!" They paid no attention to his cries, and the Wolf destroyed the entire flock.

When the people saw what happened to their sheep, they were very angry. *"There is no believing a liar,"* they said, *"even when he speaks the truth!"*

Jupiter, Neptune, Minerva, and Momus

ACCORDING to an ancient legend, the first man was made by Jupiter, the first bull by Neptune, and the first house by Minerva. The story says that, when the gods had finished their work, they argued as to which was the most perfect. Since they could not reach a satisfactory decision, they decided to appoint Momus as judge.

Now Momus was without talent himself, and so began to find fault with each. First he criticized the work of Neptune: "You have not set the horns of the bull below his eyes. How can he see where to strike?"

He then condemned the work of Jupiter: "You have not placed the heart of man outside his body. How can others see his inner thoughts and feelings?"

Lastly he attacked Minerva: "Your house has no wheels. How can its inhabitants move away if they have unpleasant neighbors?"

Angered, Jupiter took away from the faultfinding Momus the right to judge. "It is only too clear," he said to Momus, "that *he who is envious can see no greatness in the achievements of others.*"

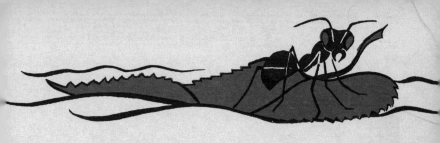

The Ant
and the Dove

A THIRSTY Ant went to the river to drink. To reach the river he had to climb down the steep bank on a blade of grass. Halfway down he slipped and fell into the swirling waters.

A Dove, perched in a nearby tree, saw the Ant's desperate plight. Quickly she plucked a leaf from the tree and dropped it into the river, close to the Ant. The Ant was able to climb up on the leaf and float safely to shore.

As soon as he was on dry land, the Ant saw a hunter of birds hiding behind a tree with a net in his hand. Seeing that the Dove was in danger, he crawled up to the hunter and bit him on his heel. The startled hunter dropped his net, and the Dove flew off.

The Dove, perched safely in the tree, called down to the Ant, "Thank you, my little friend."

"Not at all," said the Ant. *"One good turn deserves another."*

The Farmer and His Sons

AN OLD Farmer lay on his deathbed. "I would die happy," he thought, "if I could make sure that my sons would take the same good care of the farm as I have done."

He called his two sons to his bedside and said, "My sons, I have not long to live. Listen carefully to what I have to say."

The two young men bent down to catch their father's feeble words. "There is great treasure hidden in the vineyard," he whispered to them. And so saying, the old Farmer died.

The two sons began to hunt for the treasure. With their spades and plows they turned the soil of the land, but they found neither gold nor precious stones.

However, the vines were strengthened by their careful plowing, and began to yield the richest crop of grapes they had ever seen.

The oldest son turned to his brother and said, "Now I know the treasure of which our dear father spoke. It is our vineyard, which is more precious now than ever."

"Yes," the younger son said. "How wise our father was. He wanted us to learn that *hard work can often yield great riches*."

37

The Lark and Her
Young Ones

IN THE early spring a Lark made her nest in a field of young green wheat. By the time the baby Larks had grown to their full size, the wheat was quite ripe.

The Farmer looked at his field and said, "It is time to cut my wheat. I must send for my neighbors to help me."

The young Larks heard him and hurried to tell their mother. "The Farmer is going to cut the wheat," they cried. "Quick! We must move to a safe place."

"There is time enough, my children," the Mother Lark said.

A few days later the Farmer came again to their field. He saw that now the overripe wheat was almost ready to fall to the ground. "There is no time to lose," the Farmer said. "I will hire some reapers, and I will come myself tomorrow and see that the wheat is cut."

Again the young Larks told their mother what the Farmer had said.

"Now it is time to be off, my little ones," said the Mother Lark. "When a man does his work himself instead of leaving it to others, he is in earnest. Remember this, my loves, *if you want a job well done, then do it yourself!*"

The Wolf, the Lion,
and the Lamb

ONE day a Wolf stole a Lamb. He seized it from the flock and was carrying it off to his den when a Lion stepped into his path. The Lion then seized the Lamb away from the Wolf. The Wolf ran off and from a safe distance cried out to the Lion, "You have unjustly taken from me that which was mine!"

"So," peered the Lion, "it was justly yours, eh? I suppose the Lamb was a gift from a friend! You should know that *you have no right to what is not rightfully yours.*"

The Miser

ONCE there was a Miser who sold all his possessions and, with the money, bought a great lump of gold. He dug a deep hole at the edge of the garden, and there he buried his gold. Once a day thereafter the Miser went to the garden, dug up his gold, and fondled it lovingly.

One of the Miser's workmen wondered why his master spent so much time in the garden. One day he hid behind a tree and soon discovered the secret of the hidden treasure.

That night, when the Miser was fast asleep, the workman crept into the garden and stole the lump of gold.

When the Miser found that his gold was gone, he tore his hair and cried aloud in his despair. A neighbor came running to see what was the matter, and the grief-stricken Miser told her what had happened.

Then the neighbor said, "Pray stop your weeping. Go and find a stone. Place the stone in the hole and imagine that it is your lump of gold. The stone will serve your purpose, for you never meant to use the gold anyway. *To a miser, what he has is of no more use than what he has not.*"

The Lion and the Mouse

A LION was awakened from sleep by a Mouse running across his face. With a terrible roar, the Lion seized the Mouse with his paw and was about to kill him.

"Oh please," the Mouse begged. "Spare my life! I will be sure to repay your kindness."

The King of Beasts was so amused at the thought of a Mouse being able to help *him* that he let the frightened creature go.

Shortly afterward the Lion fell into a trap set by some hunters and was hopelessly caught in a strong ropes. In his misery the Lion roared so loudly that all the beasts in the forest heard him.

The Mouse recognized the roar of his former captor and ran to the place where the Lion lay trapped. At once the Mouse began to gnaw the ropes with his teeth. He gnawed rope after rope until at last the Lion was free.

"Thank you," said the grateful Lion. "I know now that *in time of need the weak may help the strong*."

The Horse and the Groom

THERE was once a Groom who used to brush his Horse with the greatest care and comb his mane for hours on end. Yet at the same time the Groom stole the Horse's corn and sold it in the village for his own profit.

One day the Horse said to the Groom, "If you really wish me to look my best, groom me less and feed me more. Though you brush my coat you steal my food, and *he who steals with a smile is none the less a scoundrel.*"

The Miller, His Son, and Their Donkey

ONE hot day a Miller and his son were taking their Donkey to a neighboring fair to sell him. They had not gone far when they met some girls on the road, talking and laughing.

"Look there!" cried one of the girls, pointing at them. "What fools you are to be trudging along this hot road while you could be riding."

So the Miller sat his son upon the Donkey and walked along by his side. Presently they came upon a group of old men who were engaged in serious conversation. One of the men looked up and said, "See that! It just proves what I was saying. No one has any respect for old age any more. Imagine that lazy boy riding while his poor old father walks! Get down, you lazy loafer, and let the old man rest his weary legs."

Hearing this, the Miller made his son dismount and got up on the Donkey's back himself. Thus they continued on their way, the son walking and the old Miller riding, until they met a group of women and children.

"Why, you horrid old man," one of the women cried. "How can you ride upon that Donkey while the poor little lad can hardly keep up with you?"

The Miller gave thought to this, and then picked

up his son and placed the boy behind him on the Donkey's back.

The Miller and his son were riding into town when a passing villager called out, "For shame! Surely that Donkey is not your own."

The Miller assured him that it was.

"I never would have thought so by the way the poor beast is loaded. Why, you two fellows do not look sick to me! Surely you are better able to carry that Donkey than the Donkey is to carry both of you!"

So the Miller and his son dismounted. They tied the Donkey's legs together with some cord and strung him over a pole. With the pole across their shoulders, they walked over a bridge that led into town.

The townsfolk had never seen such a funny sight, and they laughed loudly. The noise so frightened the poor animal that he began to wiggle and kick. The cords that bound him snapped, and the Donkey tumbled from the pole into the river.

Sadly the old Miller and his son walked all the way home, thinking, *"When you try to please everyone, you end up by pleasing no one."*

The Oxen and the Driver

A TEAM of Oxen dragged a heavy wagon along a dusty country road. Each time the wooden wheels of the wagon turned on the axles, they groaned and creaked. At last the Driver cried out in exasperation, "Wagon! Why do *you* make so much noise? It is the Oxen who are drawing all the weight, and they are silent!"

The Oxen, plodding on, heard him. One turned to the other and said, "Our master is right. *Those who suffer least often cry out the loudest.*"

The Wizard

A WIZARD was well known for telling the fortunes of those who passed by in the market place. One afternoon a man ran up to him in great haste and cried, "Wizard! A thief has broken into your home. At this moment all your possessions are being stolen. Make haste!"

The Wizard jumped up in alarm and hurried from the market place. A townsman saw him running and cried out, "Wizard, you foretell the fortunes of others. Pray, how is it that you did not foresee this misfortune of your own?"

The Wizard called back as he ran on, "*It is far easier to be wise for others than for ourselves.*"

The Mischievous Dog

THERE was once a Dog so ill-behaved and mischievous that he used to creep up to the townsfolk and bite them before they knew what was happening.

Much angered, his master hung a bell around the Dog's neck to warn the people of his presence. At first the Dog was irked by the noisy bell. Then he grew proud of it, and after a while he paraded around in the market place showing it off.

Finally an old Hound said to him, "Why do you make such a show of yourself? You act as if the bell around your neck were an honor. Don't you realize it is a disgrace — a sign to all men to avoid you? You don't seem to know the difference, so let me tell you *that to be widely known is not necessarily to be admired!*

The Old Woman and the Physician

AN old woman who had lost the use of her eyes called in a physician.

"Cure me of my blindness," the old woman said, "and I will pay you well. But if I remain blind, I will pay you nothing. Do you agree?"

The physician consented to the bargain. He came to her house each week and applied some worthless salve to her eyes. But each time he quietly carried a piece of furniture away with him. This went on until he had stolen all her possessions.

Then the physician gave her a salve that cured her, and the old woman could see again. Now that she had recovered her sight, she saw that her house was bare, and therefore she would pay him nothing.

The physician insisted that she pay him, but the old woman refused. At last the physician took her to court.

The old woman stood before the judge and said, "This man speaks the truth. I did agree to pay him well if I recovered my sight. He agreed I need pay him nothing if I remained blind. Now he says that I am healed. I say I am still blind, for when I lost the use of my eyes my house was filled with fine furniture and goods, yet now I am not able to see any of it!"

The judge settled the case in favor of the old

woman, saying, *"Those who are so ready to take what is not their own must be prepared to lose what is theirs."*

The Playful Donkey

A MONKEY climbed up to the roof of a building and jumped and danced about. The owner of the building laughed and praised his amusing performance. The next day a Donkey climbed to the roof, and while he was dancing about he broke a large part of the roof. The owner of the building went up after him and quickly drove him down with a thick wooden club.

"Why do you beat me so severely?" the Donkey groaned. "Why, the Monkey did the very same thing yesterday, and all you did was laugh!"

"That is quite true," the owner said. "But you must realize *that what is right for one may be quite wrong for another.*"

The Fox and the Stork

A FOX invited a Stork to dinner and slyly served the Stork nothing but thin soup in a very shallow dish. The Fox lapped up his soup easily, but the poor Stork could only wet the end of her bill. She left the Fox's house as hungry as she had arrived.

"I am so sorry," said the Fox with a crafty smile, "that my soup was not to your liking. Perhaps it was not seasoned enough?"

"Oh, do not apologize," said the Stork. "Would you do me the honor of dining with me next week?"

The Fox consented and arrived at the Stork's house, looking forward to a good meal. But to his disappointment he saw that the soup was served in a long jar with a narrow mouth.

The Stork thrust her long neck and bill into the jar and thoroughly enjoyed her dinner. The Fox could only lick a few drops around the neck of the bottle. But he did not dare to find fault with the Stork. He understood only too well that *he who tricks others must expect to be tricked.*

The Lion and the Bulls

A LION prowled about in a pasture where four Bulls were grazing. He tried many times to capture them, but each time he failed. Whenever he came near, the four Bulls turned and formed a ring, so that no matter which way the Lion approached, he was met by their horns.

One day, however, the Bulls had a quarrel and would not speak to one another. Each went alone to a separate part of the pasture to graze. This was the moment the Lion had been waiting for. One by one he attacked the Bulls and made an end of them.

Well fed and contented, the Lion thought, "Those beasts would still be grazing had they remembered: *United we stand; divided we fall.*"

The Milkmaid and Her Pail

A MILKMAID was on her way to market. On her head she carried a large pail of milk. As she walked along she thought of all the money she would have as soon as she sold the milk.

"I shall buy hens from Farmer Brown," she thought, "and they will lay eggs every day. I will sell the eggs to the parson's wife. She will pay me well. With the money from the eggs, I will buy myself a new frock and bonnet. What color shall they be? I think green — a lovely green, for that color becomes me best. When I go to market, I will wear my new clothes. All the young men will want to speak to me, of course, but I shall pretend not to see them. When they follow me, I shall walk proudly on. I'll toss my head — like this." And with that, she tossed her head. The pail slipped off from her head, and the milk spilled all over the ground.

The Milkmaid brought her empty pail and her sad tale home to her mother. "Ah, my daughter," said her mother, *"do not count your chickens before they are hatched."*

The Wolf
and the Lamb

ONE day a Wolf met a Lamb who had strayed from the fold. The Wolf resolved not to kill the Lamb without a good excuse that would justify his right to eat him.

So he said, "Ah, you are the Lamb who insulted me so harshly last year."

"Indeed no," bleated the Lamb. "A year ago I was not yet born."

The Wolf tried again. "Then you must be the Lamb that feeds in my pasture."

"No, good sir," the Lamb protested, "I have not yet tasted grass."

"Well," snapped the Wolf, "then you are the Lamb who drinks from my well."

"No!" exclaimed the Lamb, "I have no need of water, for my mother's milk is both food and drink to me."

Seizing the Lamb, the Wolf snarled, "I will have my supper — even though you deny everyone of my accusations!" As the Lamb struggled to be free, he thought, "*Any excuse will serve a tyrant.*"

The Mice in Council

ONE day the Mice called a meeting to discuss how they might best outwit their enemy, the Cat. They talked for hours, but could not find a good plan.

At last a young Mouse stood up with an air of great importance. "We all know," said he, "that it is the sly way in which our enemy approaches us that is our greatest danger. I propose that a bell be hung around the neck of the Cat. Then we will always know when she is coming, and we will have time to hide."

The Mice were very excited at this idea. "How clever!" they said. "At last we have found a way."

But then a wise old Mouse, who had sat silent, stood up to speak. "Yes," he said slowly, "that is indeed a wonderful plan. We will surely be safe. When the bell tinkles on the neck of the Cat, we will have time to run. But tell me this — which one of us is going to put the bell on the Cat?"

The Mice looked from one to another, and no one spoke. Then the old Mouse shook his head sadly and said, "Yes my friends, *many things are easier said than done.*"

The Trumpeter Taken Prisoner

THERE was once a Trumpeter who liked to ride at the head of the troops, blowing his trumpet proudly. One day in battle he was the first to be taken prisoner by the enemy.

He cried out to his captors, "Pray spare me. I have not killed a single man in your army. Indeed I have no weapons. See — the only thing I carry is this harmless brass trumpet."

"That is the very reason why you should die," his captor replied. "While you do not fight yourself, your trumpet stirs up all the others to battle. *He who incites others to war is worse than he who fights.*"

The Horse, the Hunter, and the Stag

A HORSE roamed freely on the great plain. Then one day a Stag came to the plain, and the Horse had to share the land on which he grazed.

"This is my plain," said the Horse. But the Stag refused to leave. The angry Horse wished to take revenge, and asked a passing Hunter to help him punish the Stag. The Hunter said, "I can only catch the fleet-footed Stag with your help. You must let me put this iron bit in your mouth so that I may guide you with these reins. And you must let me put this saddle on your back so that I may sit steady as we pursue the enemy."

The Horse agreed and was soon bridled and saddled. The Hunter sprang into the saddle, and together they chased the Stag from the plains.

Then the Horse said to the Hunter, "Thank you for your help. Now if you will kindly remove the iron bit from my mouth and the heavy saddle from my back, I shall be on my way."

"Not so fast, friend Horse," said the Hunter. "You are in my power now, and from this moment on you must serve man!"

There was nothing the poor Horse could do but reflect sadly that *freedom is too high a price to pay for revenge.*

The Sick Lion

AN OLD Lion, who was no longer able to provide himself with food by force, turned to trickery. He made it known that he was very sick and would welcome any visitors who might care to call on him in his cave.

The beasts heard the news. One by one they came to his cave to express their sympathy. And one by one the Lion devoured them. After many of the beasts had disappeared in this way, the Fox discovered the Lion's trickery. He stopped at a safe distance from the cave and called to the Lion, "How are you feeling today, Your Majesty?"

"I seem to be a little better," the Lion replied. "But why do you stand outside? Pray enter and visit with me."

"No thank you," said the Fox. "I notice that there are many footprints that lead into your cave, but none that lead out. I discovered long ago that *the wise can learn from the misfortunes of others.*"

The Salt Peddler and
the Donkey

A SALT PEDDLER drove his Donkey to the seashore to buy salt. He loaded baskets of salt on the Donkey's back and started home. On the way they passed a stream. The Donkey lost his footing and fell into the water. When he emerged from the stream, he found his load much lighter, for much of the salt had dissolved in the water.

Once more the Peddler returned to the seashore, refilled his baskets with salt, and continued home. When the Donkey came to the stream, he fell again. But this time he fell on purpose.

The Peddler understood what the Donkey was up to, but he said nothing. Instead he drove the Donkey to the seashore once again. This time, however, he bought a cargo of sponges and loaded them upon the Donkey's back.

When they came back to the stream, the Donkey again made sure that he fell in. But the sponges became swollen with water, and instead of lightening his burden the Donkey found he had doubled it.

The Peddler chuckled and said to the Donkey, "A trick can work both ways, you know, *and two can play the same game.*"

The Hare and the Tortoise

ONE day the Hare was boasting, as usual, of his amazing speed.

"No one can run faster than I," he bragged to the other animals. "I'm swifter than the wind. I challenge anyone here to run a race with me."

None of the animals seemed ready to accept the challenge. "What?" said the Hare. "Will no one dare to race with me?"

"I will," said a quiet voice. It was the Tortoise.

"You!" the Hare exclaimed. "Surely you must be joking. How can *you* hope to win?"

"We shall see," said the Tortoise calmly. "Let us race."

It was agreed that they would race through the woods and back. The signal was given, and the Hare hopped out of sight at once, while the Tortoise plodded slowly along.

Soon the Hare was so far ahead of the Tortoise that he stopped to rest on the soft grass. "To think that a Tortoise would want to race with me!" thought the Hare, laughing to himself. "Why I even have time for a nap." And he curled up on the soft grass and went to sleep.

Meanwhile the Tortoise plodded steadily on — and on and on. After a while he passed the Hare, who was still asleep. Just as the Tortoise came to the finish line, the Hare awoke and saw where the Tortoise was. The Hare made a great leap forward, but it was too late. The Tortoise had won the race.

As the Hare crept away, shamefaced, he heard the animals exclaim, "You won! You won! How did you ever beat the Hare?"

Modestly, the Tortoise told them, "*Slow and steady wins the race.*"

The Bundle of Sticks

A FATHER had a family of sons who were always quarreling among themselves. He tried in every way to teach them to get along, but still they quarreled. Then one day he called his sons together and showed them a bundle of sticks. He asked each of them in turn to break the bundle. Each son tried with all his strength, but not one could even bend it. Then the father untied the bundle and separated the sticks.

To each of his sons he gave a stick. "Now try," he said. And each son broke his stick easily.

Then the father said, "My sons, if you remain united you will be as strong as this bundle of sticks. But if you are divided among yourselves, you will be broken as easily as you have broken the sticks. Know that *in union there is strength*."

The Travelers and the Bear

TWO men were traveling together when a Bear suddenly came out of the forest and stood in their path, growling. One of the men quickly climbed the nearest tree and concealed himself in the branches. The other man, seeing that there was no time to hide, fell flat on the ground. He pretended to be dead, for he had heard it said that a Bear will not touch a dead man.

The Bear came near, sniffed the man's head and body, and then lumbered away, back into the forest.

When the Bear was out of sight, the man in the tree slid down and said to his friend, "I saw the Bear whispering to you. What did he have to say?"

The other man replied, "The Bear told me never to travel with a friend who deserts me at the first sign of danger." He looked his companion straight in the eye. "The Bear said that, *in time of trouble, one learns who his true friends are.*"

The Lion in Love

IN DAYS of old, a Lion fell in love with a Woodsman's beautiful daughter and asked for her hand in marriage. The Woodsman was unwilling to grant the Lion's request. Yet he was afraid to anger the King of Beasts.

"Noble Lion," the Woodsman said, "I am greatly honored by your proposal. But, sir, have you considered my daughter's fears? Your great teeth and your sharp claws terrify her. Before you can be a suitable bridegroom for my daughter, you must let me cut off your claws and take out your teeth."

The Lion was too deeply in love to protest. So he consented, and the deed was done.

The Lion then demanded that the Woodsman's daughter become his bride at once. But the Woodsman was no longer afraid of the Lion, for the great beast now had neither teeth nor claws.

With his heavy club the Woodsman set upon the Lion and drove him into the forest.

"Alas!" cried the Lion, *"Now I know that those in love really take leave of their senses."*

The Wolf in Sheep's Clothing

ONE day a Wolf found the skin of a sheep. He put it on and said to himself, "Now I can graze with the sheep and choose the plumpest ones for my dinner, and no one will be the wiser."

So well did the sheepskin disguise him that no one was suspicious when the Wolf took his place among the flock. A little later the Shepherd came to the fold to choose a sheep for his supper. He reached in and seized the Wolf, thinking he was one of the sheep. Only when he had killed the Wolf did the shepherd realize his mistake. "Ah," he said, *"those who intend harm often come to harm themselves."*

The Fisherman and the Little Fish

A FISHERMAN was fishing all day and caught only one small fish. The fish begged for his life, saying, "Pray spare me and put me back into the sea. I shall soon become a large fish, fit for the tables of the rich. Then you can catch me again and make a handsome profit."

The fisherman shook his head and said, "I should indeed be a very simple fellow if I gave up today's certain gain for tomorrow's uncertain profit. *A small fish caught is better than a large one in the sea."*

The Fox and the Crow

A HUNGRY Crow stole a piece of cheese and flew with it onto the branch of a tree. Just as she was about to take the first bite, a sly Fox spied her and called from below.

"Good day, Mistress Crow, how well you are looking! How glossy your feathers, how shining your eyes! I am certain that your voice is lovely, too. Oh, if I could hear but one song from you I would surely greet you as the Queen of Birds."

The Crow, who was very vain, believed every word spoken by the Fox. Fluttering her wings, she lifted her head and opened her mouth to caw. With that, the cheese dropped to the ground and was immediately snapped up by the Fox.

As he walked away, well fed and well pleased with his cleverness, the Fox called back to the Crow, "In exchange for that delicious cheese, I will give you a bit of advice: *Remember not to trust those who praise you falsely.*"

The Trees and the Ax

A WOODSMAN came into the forest and asked the Trees to provide him with a handle for his ax.

Some of the Trees, wishing to save themselves, told the Woodsman where he could find a very young Ash Tree. The Woodsman then pulled the Ash Tree out of the ground.

No sooner had the Woodsman carved the Ash Tree into a sturdy handle than he began to use his ax. He set to work right and left, felling the noblest giants of the forest.

An old Oak, mourning the destruction of the mighty trees which had been his friends, said to a Cedar Tree nearby, "If we had not given up the Ash Tree to please the Woodsman, we all might have stood for hundreds of years."

"Yes," said the Cedar Tree sadly. "We should have known that *if we want our own lives protected, we must protect the lives of others.*"

The Boy and the Nuts

A BOY, seeing a pitcher full of walnuts, thrust his hand in to get some. He grasped as many as he could hold, and then tried to pull out his hand. But his fist was bulging with the walnuts, and he could not get it out of the pitcher. Unwilling to give up any of the walnuts but unable to draw out his hand, the boy burst into tears.

A bystander saw him crying and said, "If you will be satisfied with fewer nuts, you will be able to get your hand free. *It is better to be content with half than to lose all.*"

The Boy Who Swam in the River

O NE warm spring day, a boy was walking along the bank of a river. The water looked so inviting that he took off his clothes and dived in. But the river current was very strong, and soon the boy was in danger of drowning. Just then a traveler came by. He saw the boy struggling and began to scold him for going swimming in the river so early in the season.

"Oh, sir!" cried the boy, "pray help me now and scold me afterward. At a time like this, *advice without action is useless.*"

The Frogs Who Desired a King

THE Frogs were happy all day long playing in their marshy swamp. They splashed and jumped without a care in the world. But one day a few of the Frogs began to think there was something wrong with their easy way of life.

They said, "We should have a King. Then he would tell us what to do."

The Frogs made this request of Jupiter. He laughed at them and said, "Very well, you sillies! Here is your King!" And he threw down a log.

At first the Frogs were terrified at the great splash the log made, and they hid amid the tall rushes. Then one by one they swam up to it, touched it, climbed on it, and jumped up and down to their heart's content.

"This King does not move!" the Frogs complained to Jupiter. "We want a real King, one who will really rule over us."

Jupiter was angered at the stupidity of the Frogs. "Very well, I will send you a King who *does* move." And he sent them a stork who at once began to gobble up the Frogs.

"Save us, Jupiter," cried the Frogs, as they tried to escape from the Stork.

"No," said Jupiter scornfully. "You will have to make the best of what you asked for, since you were not content to *let well enough alone*."

The Goose
With the Golden Eggs

ONE morning a Farmer was astonished to discover that his Goose had laid an egg of solid gold. He seized the precious egg, ran into the house, and with trembling hands showed it to his wife. "Look, my wife," he said, "we are rich!" Then the Farmer took the golden egg to market and sold it for a good price. The next morning the goose again laid a golden egg, and the Farmer sold that too for much money. Every day thereafter the Farmer found in the barnyard an egg of purest gold. One by one he sold the eggs and soon became a very rich man. But the richer he became, the more money he wanted.

One day he thought, "Why must I be content with only one golden egg a day? If I kill the goose and cut her open, I can take all the treasure at once!"

Whereupon he seized his ax and killed the goose —but alas, there was no gold at all inside.

"Foolish man!" cried his wife. "If only you had understood that *those who are greedy for too much sometimes lose all.*"

The Wolf and the Crane

ONCE when a Wolf was eating supper, a bone stuck in his throat. Almost choking to death, the Wolf begged a Crane to put her head into his throat and draw out the bone. "I will reward you generously," the Wolf promised.

It took the Crane only a few minutes to pull out the bone. But when he asked for the reward, the Wolf laughed at him.

"Were you not able to pull your head safely out of my jaw? Is that not payment enough!"

"I should have known," thought the Crane, as he flew off." "*When one serves the wicked, one should expect no reward.*"

The Rooster and the Jewel

ONE spring day a hungry Rooster was scratching for food in the dirt. Suddenly his claws dug into something hard, and there on the ground he saw a glittering jewel.

"Ah," sighed the Rooster, "how happy the owner would be had he been the one to find this jewel. He would pick it up eagerly and prize it greatly. But alas, I have found this jewel for no purpose. For I would far rather have one kernel of corn than all the jewels in the world. Truly, *what has value for one is worthless to another.*"

The Gnat and the Bull

A GNAT settled on the horn of a Bull and sat there a long time. Then he buzzed into the ear of the Bull and said, "Pardon me, but has my weight been a burden to you? You have only to say so, and I will fly away and not bother you any longer."

"Oh," said the Bull. "To tell the truth I did not even know you were there, so it is all the same to me whether you go or stay. You know, *we are not always as important as we think we are.*"

The Oak and the Reeds

A LARGE Oak was uprooted one day by the violent winds of a hurricane. The great tree was thrown across a stream, where it lay amid some Reeds.

Sadly the Oak said, "Here I lie, overturned by the strong winds. Yet you Reeds, so light and weak, are still upright. How is that possible?"

"You, Sir Oak, fight against the mighty wind," the Reeds replied. "You are too proud to bend a little, and so in the end you are destroyed. But we bow before the gentlest breeze, and so we still stand. We have learned what you have not: *it is far better to bend than to break.*"

The Monkey and the Dolphin

A SAILOR, embarking on a voyage to Greece, took along a Monkey to amuse him on shipboard. Off the coast of Greece, near Athens, a violent storm arose. Angry waves beat against the ship and dashed it to pieces. The Sailor, his Monkey, and all the crew jumped into the sea and swam for their lives.

A Dolphin saw the Monkey struggling in the water, came to his assistance, and swam with the Monkey on his back toward the shore. Then the Dolphin, thinking the Monkey was a man, asked, "Are you, sir, an Athenian?"

"Certainly I am," the Monkey replied, "and furthermore I am descended from one of the noblest families of Athens."

"Then of course you know Piraeus," the Dolphin said.

The Monkey did not know that Piraeus was the famous harbor of Athens. "Oh yes," he said, "I know Piraeus very well. He is one of my closest friends."

The Dolphin was so angered at these lies that he dove into the water and swam away, leaving the Monkey to flounder helplessly in the sea. Then he called back to the Monkey, *"Those who tell falsehoods sooner or later find themselves in deep water."*

The Lioness

THE beasts of field and forest were arguing as to which of the animals produced the greatest number of young ones.

Just then a Lioness passed by. The beasts stopped her and said, "We are trying to find out who among us has the most offspring. Pray tell us, madam, how many cubs are born to you at one time?"

The Lioness smiled and answered, "Only one, but pray remember, he is a *Lion! Value is in worth, not in number*."

About Aesop

AESOP was a slave who lived in Greece about 3000 years ago. He became famous for the clever animal fables through which he showed the wise and foolish behavior of men.

Not much is really known about the life of Aesop. It is said that his wisdom so delighted one of his masters that the slave was given his freedom. It is said, too, that he became an honored guest at the courts of kings.

Aesop's fables have become a part of our daily language — a way of expressing ourselves. Haven't you heard people talk about "sour grapes" or "not counting chickens until they are hatched"?

Aesop never wrote down his stories. He told them to people, who in turn told them to others. Not until 200 years after his death did the first collection of his fables appear. Since then they have been translated into almost every language in the world. Today there are many, many versions of the tales that Aesop told in the hills of Greece so long ago.

APPLE Classics

☐ MA43880-8	**Aesop's Fables** Ann McGovern	**$2.99**
☐ MA42035-6	**Alice in Wonderland** Lewis Carroll	**$3.50**
☐ MA44556-1	**Anne of Avonlea** L. M. Montgomery	**$4.50**
☐ MA42243-X	**Anne of Green Gables** L. M. Montgomery	**$2.95**
☐ MA46163-X	**Anne of the Island** L. M. Montgomery	**$3.25**
☐ MA43053-X	**Around the World in Eighty Days** Jules Verne	**$4.50**
☐ MA43527-2	**A Christmas Carol** Charles Dickens	**$3.50**
☐ MA42520-X	**Five Little Peppers and How They Grew** Margaret Sidney	**$3.99**
☐ MA41295-7	**Hans Brinker and the Silver Skates** Mary Mapes Dodge	**$3.99**
☐ MA42046-1	**Heidi** Johanna Spyri	**$3.25**
☐ MA44016-0	**The Invisible Man** H. G. Wells	**$3.99**
☐ MA50323-5	**The Jungle Book** Rudyard Kipling	**$3.50**
☐ MA41279-5	**Little Men** Louisa May Alcott	**$3.99**
☐ MA54307-5	**A Little Princess** Frances Hodgson Burnett	**$3.99**
☐ MA43797-6	**Little Women** Louisa May Alcott	**$3.25**
☐ MA44769-6	**Pollyanna** Eleanor H. Porter	**$3.50**
☐ MA44025-X	**The Princess and the Goblin** George MacDonald	**$2.95**
☐ MA45260-6	**The Raven and Other Poems** Edgar Allan Poe	**$2.95**
☐ MA45441-2	**Robin Hood of Sherwood Forest** Ann McGovern	**$3.50**
☐ MA43285-0	**Robinson Crusoe** Daniel Defoe	**$4.50**
☐ MA42323-1	**Sara Crewe** Frances Hodgson Burnett	**$3.50**
☐ MA43346-6	**The Secret Garden** Frances Hodgson Burnett	**$3.50**
☐ MA44014-4	**Swiss Family Robinson** Johann Wyss	**$3.99**
☐ MA44774-2	**The Wind in the Willows** Kenneth Grahame	**$4.50**
☐ MA44089-6	**The Wizard of Oz** L. Frank Baum	**$2.95**
☐ MA46030-7	**Wuthering Heights** Emily Brönte	**$3.50**

Available wherever you buy books, or use this order form.

Scholastic Inc., P.O. Box 7502, East McCarty Street, Jefferson City, MO 65102

Please send me the books I have checked above. I am enclosing $_____ (please add $2.00 to cover shipping and handling). Send check or money order—no cash or C.O.D.s please.

Name_____

Address_____

City_____ State/Zip_____

Please allow four to six weeks for delivery. Available in the U.S. only. Sorry, mail orders are not available to residents of Canada. Prices subject to change.

AC496